WHAT IS CANCER?
Kids Book About Cancer

BABY PROFESSOR
EDUCATION KIDS

Speedy Publishing LLC

40 E. Main St. #1156

Newark, DE 19711

www.speedypublishing.com

Copyright 2016

learning about cancer

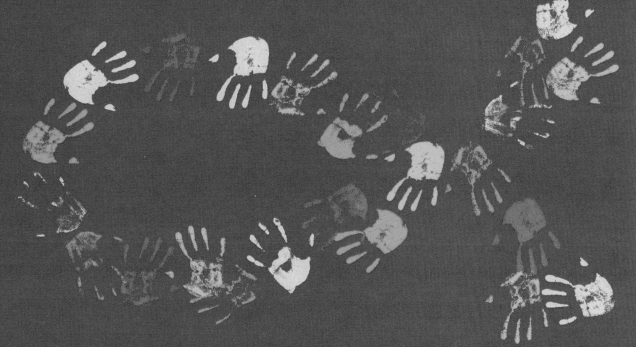

Our bodies are made up of millions of tiny cells. They are always busy doing their jobs and dividing (splitting) to make new cells. Your skin, for example, loses skin cells all day long and replaces them with new ones.

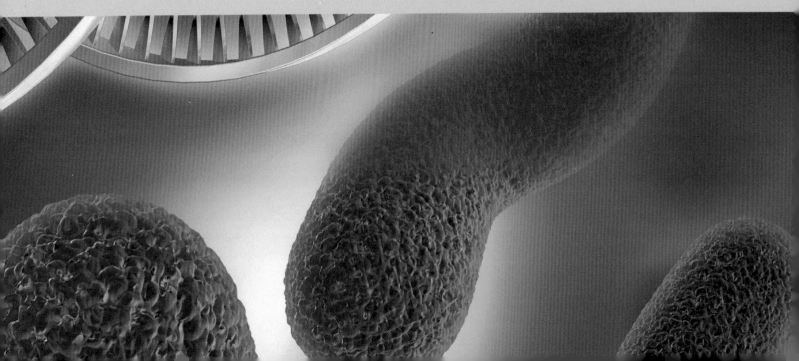

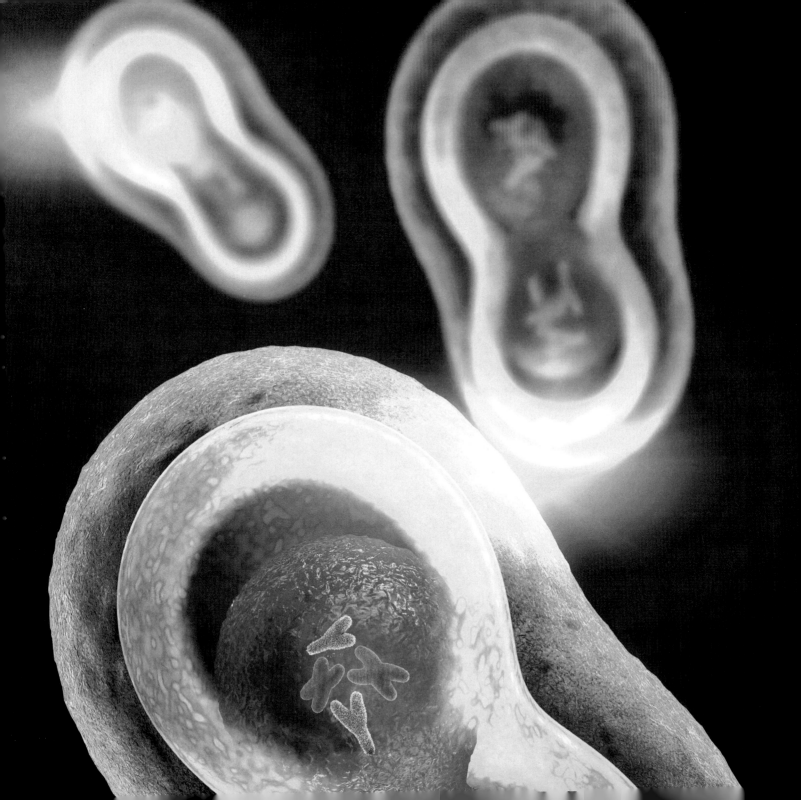

New cells are made as needed in each part of the body. Inside each cell are chemicals that give the signals for making new cells or to stop making new cells. This process is called the cell cycle.

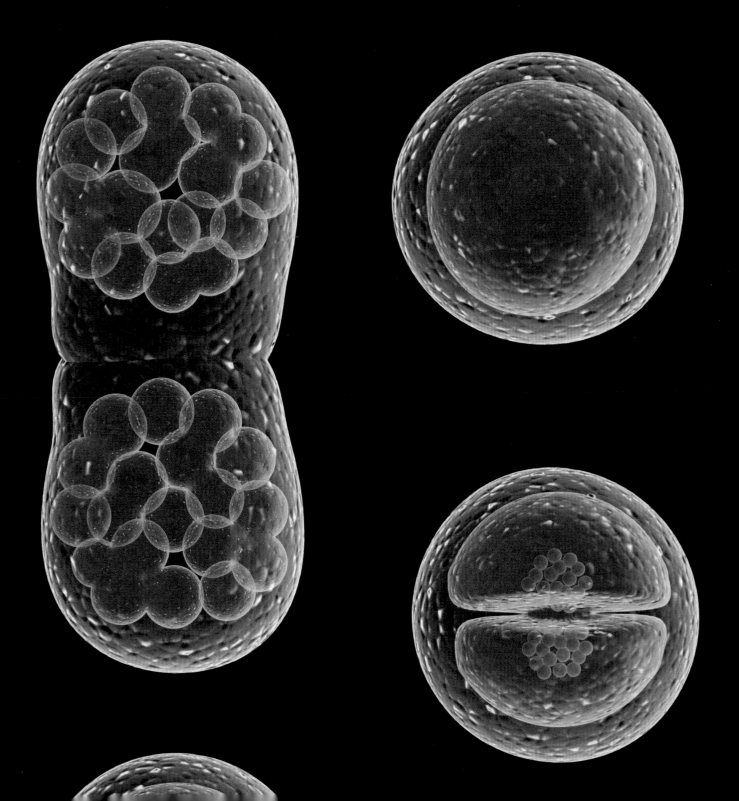

When cells get their messages mixed up, cells made are not normal cells. And when cells don't get a message to stop making new cells, too many cells are made. When the cell cycle is uncontrolled, the result is a mass growth or a tumor.

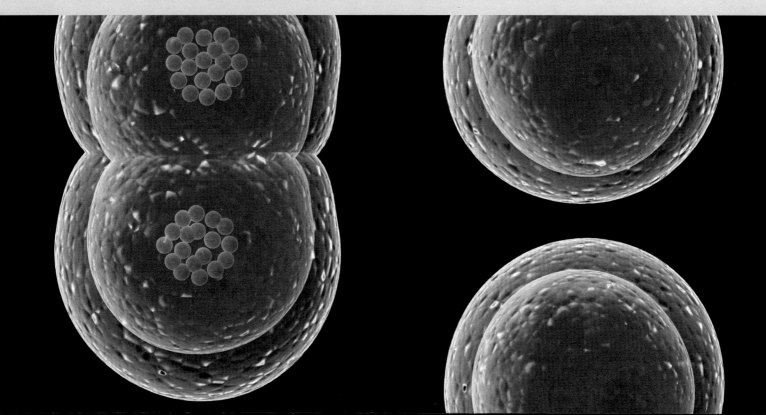

These growths are either benign or malignant. Doctors look carefully to figure out if a growth is malignant, because that is where cancer forms.

Benign means non-cancerous. Benign tumors are hardly life threatening and do not spread to other parts of the body. They can be removed easily and safely.

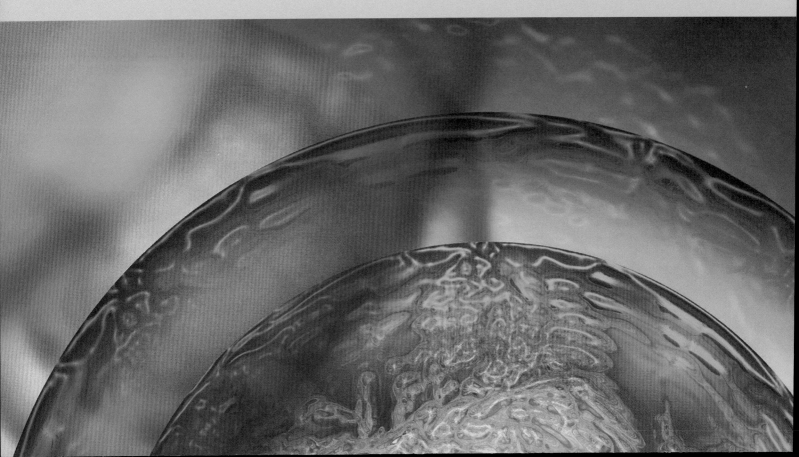

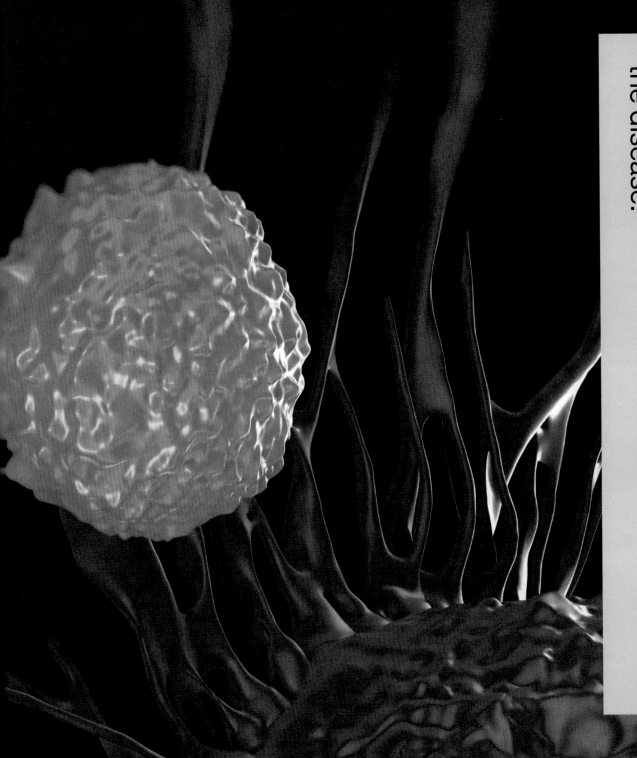

Malignant means cancerous. A malignant tumor often invades nearby tissue and organs, spreading the disease.

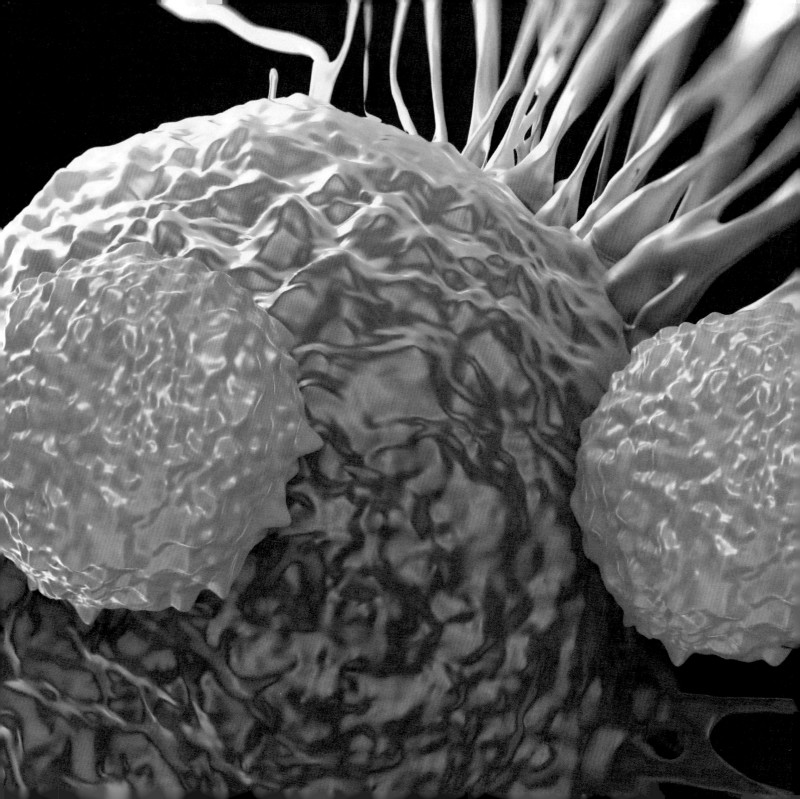

The cells in malignant tumors have the ability to attack neighboring tissues and organs. If cancerous cells break free from the area of the tumor and enter the bloodstream, spreading the disease to other organs, it called metastasis.

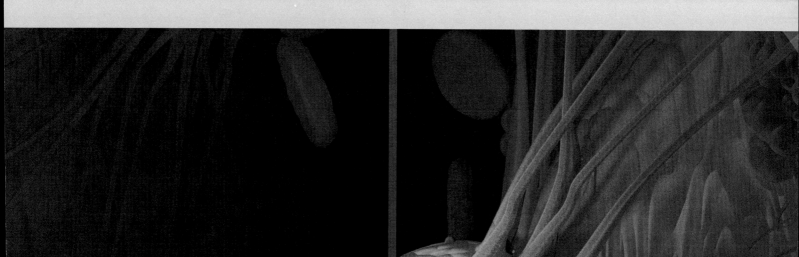

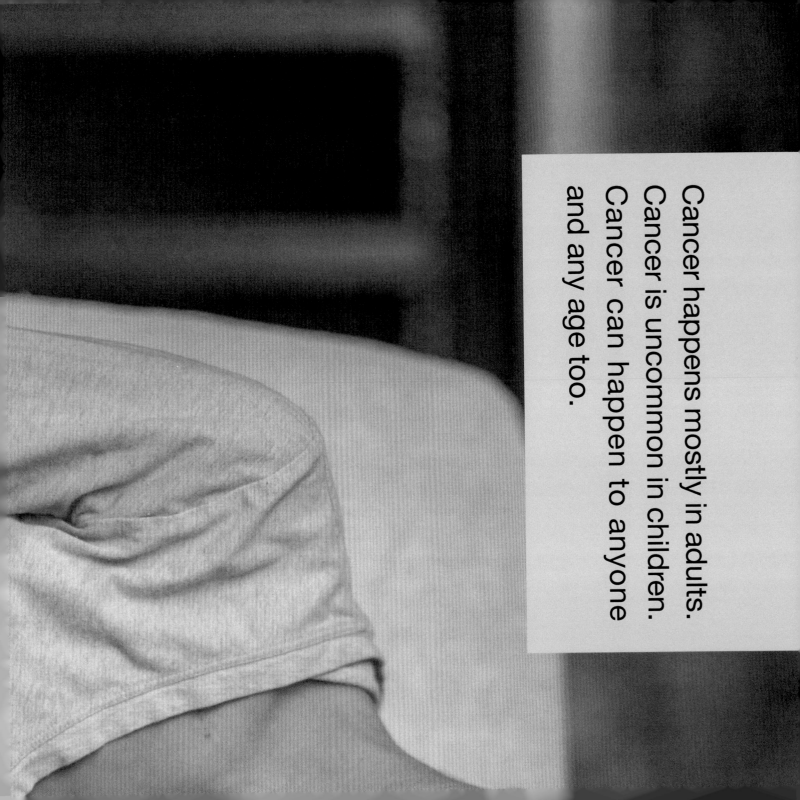

Cancer happens mostly in adults.
Cancer is uncommon in children.
Cancer can happen to anyone
and any age too.

Cancer takes away our body's strength. It destroys organs and bones. Cancer weakens the body's defenses against other illnesses.

Each cancer type is different and that means what causes cancer varies, too. There are many types of cancer and it depends on the activity of the person and its body.

We can get cancer through genes. Everyone inherits genes from their parents. If you inherit an abnormal gene (called a mutation), there is a 10% chance for an abnormal gene to result in a cancer formation.

Smoking, or sharing space with smokers, can lead to lung cancer. Tobacco smoke has more than 7,000 chemical compounds; some of these chemicals are known to be harmful, and known to cause cancer.

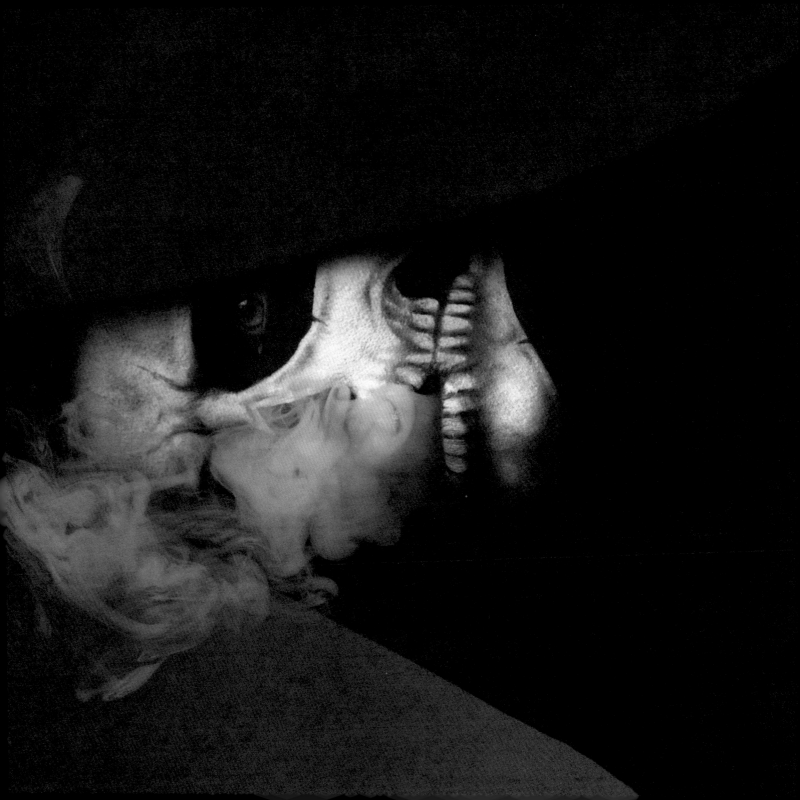

Secondhand smoke is a known human carcinogen. It comes from both the smoke that smokers puff out and the smoke of the cigarette. It may look pretty harmless, but secondhand smoke also contains thousands of chemicals that can be toxic to our body.

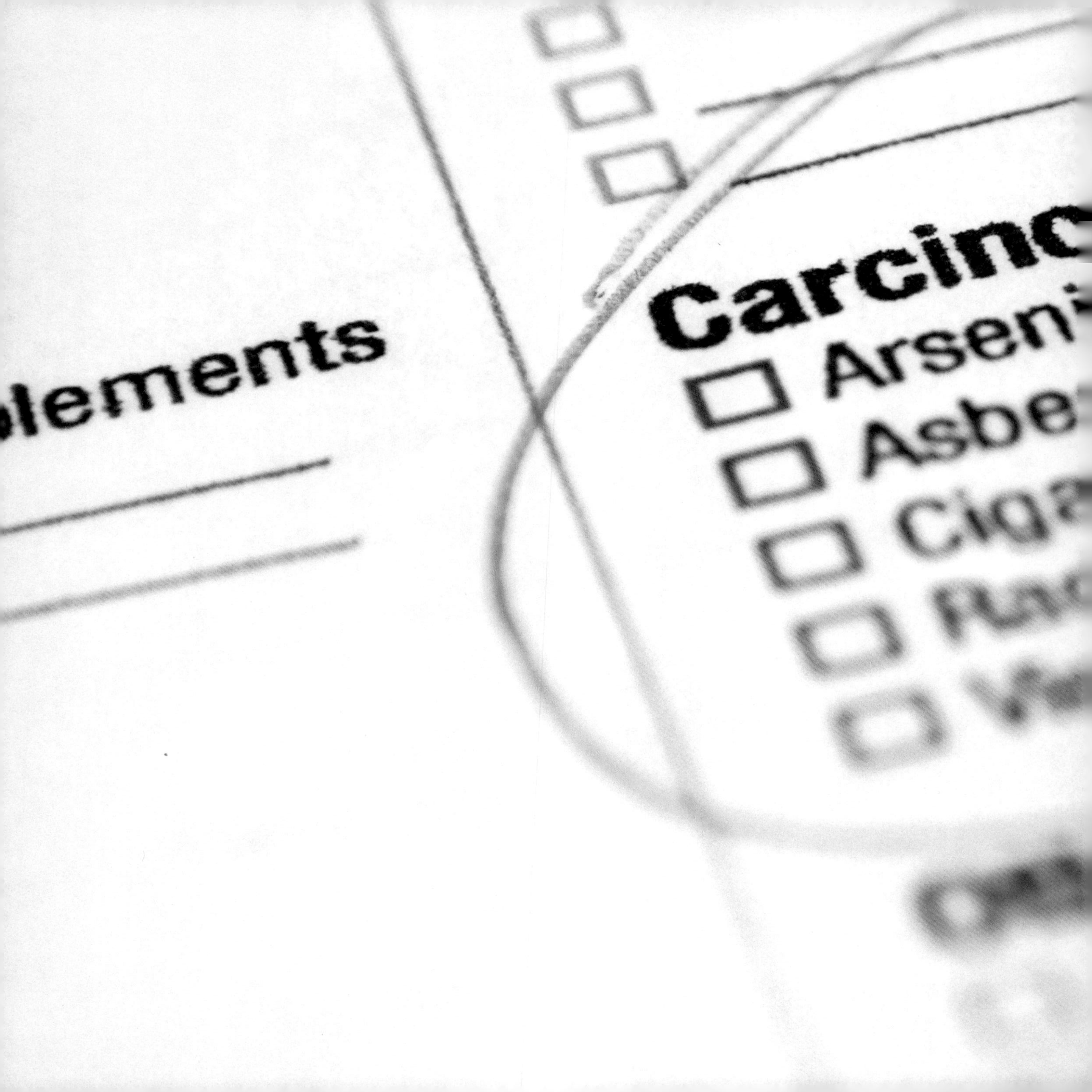

elements

Carcino

Arseni

Asbe

Ciga

Fun

Carcinogens (car-sin-o-jens) are cancer-causing agents. They are found in our environment. They come from both natural and man-made substances. We can get carcinogens from radiation and from chemicals in food.

Alcohol can lead to some types of cancer, especially when too much is consumed. Many cancer-forming chemicals are found in alcohol. It also affects our hormone levels and may damage our cells.

Anyone who has problems with their immune system is more likely to get some types of cancer. Those who do not have a strong immune system are at risk. Viruses attacking your cells are able to divide without control and can usually make use of any genetic faults they can find.

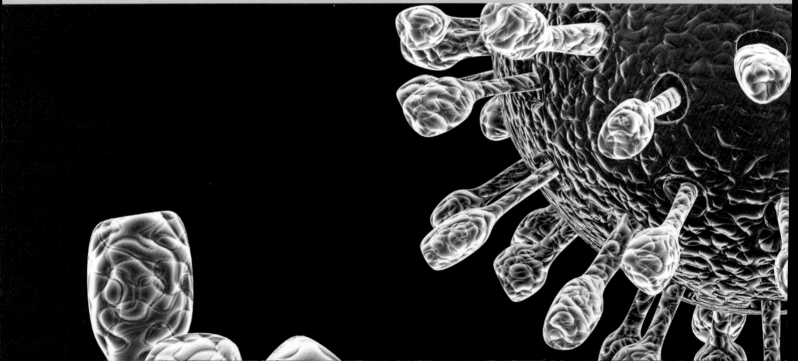

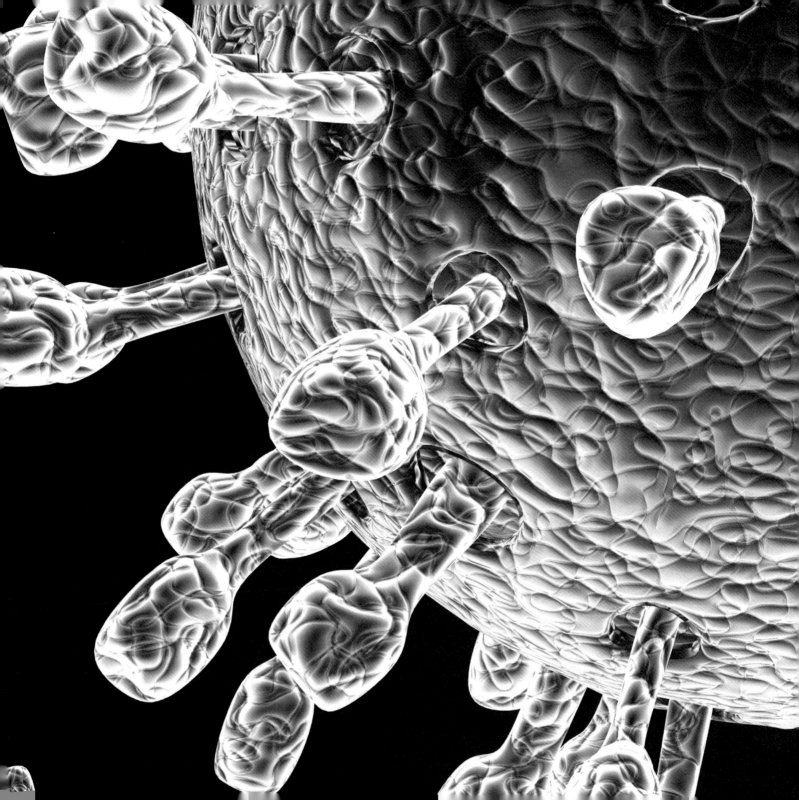

We all need some sun exposure. The sun is the top source of vitamin D that helps our bodies absorb calcium for stronger, healthier bones. But spending too much time in the sun can lead to skin cancer. There are harmful rays from the sun which can cause damage to our skin.

Many people, especially in the western world eat too much red meat and processed food, and not enough fresh fruit and vegetables. This eating habit is known to increase the risk of cancer.

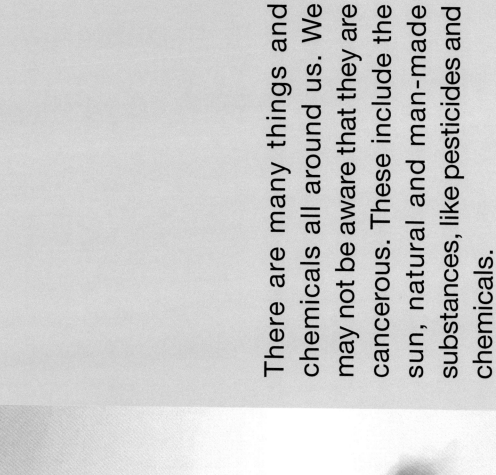

There are many things and chemicals all around us. We may not be aware that they are cancerous. These include the sun, natural and man-made substances, like pesticides and chemicals.

There are more than 200 different types of cancer. Remember we said it is a disease of the cells and cells make up tissues, and tissues make up organs. It means cancer can affect all of our body organs.

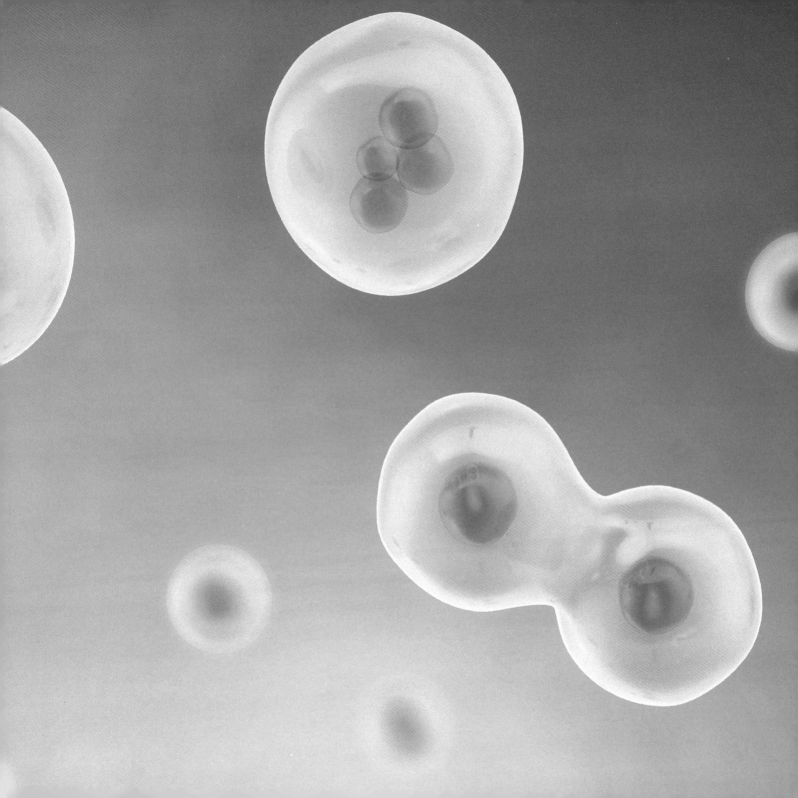

Symptoms of cancer are different and are based on the type of cancer. As cancer develops to an advanced stage, there are common symptoms which include weight loss, fever and fatigue.

Cancer is a bit complicated and no one thing is known to cause it. Cancer can happen to anyone. But it's not anyone's fault if it does.

Getting exercise and enough sleep, eating a balanced diet of good food, avoiding dangerous chemicals, and staying away from cigarette smoke reduces the risk of cancer.

Cancer can be life threatening. The solution is early diagnosis. If cancer is detected early, there is a high chance that the person can be completely cured.

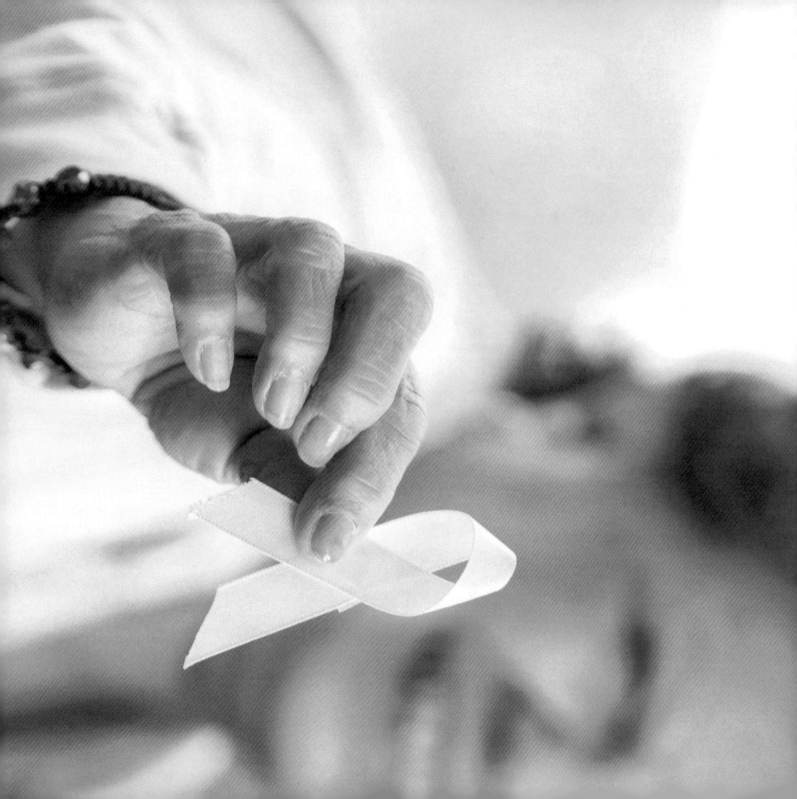

Most cancers can be treated and usually the person can have a complete recovery. Sometimes treatment can only make a person better for a short time. Treatments sometimes make people feel very sick for a while.

Surgery, chemotherapy, radiotherapy, and immunotherapy or biologic therapy are the four standard methods for cancer treatment.

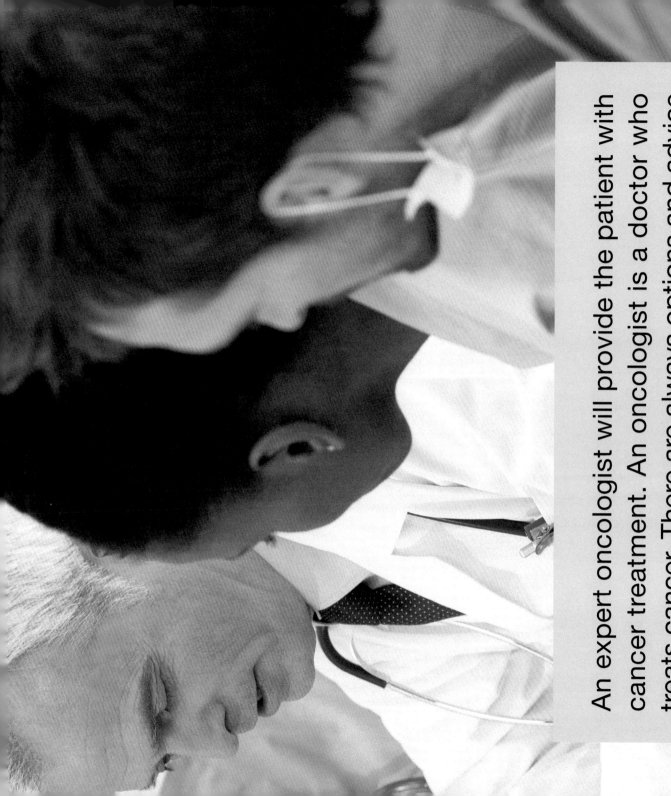

An expert oncologist will provide the patient with cancer treatment. An oncologist is a doctor who treats cancer. There are always options and advice after diagnosis of the cancer.

Meditation, special diets, counseling and exercise are some other ways of treating cancer. These treatments help the bodies and minds feel peaceful and happier so that the body may be more able to heal itself.

A person's risk to cancer can be prevented living a healthy lifestyle. Balanced diet and good exercise.

Made in the USA
Middletown, DE
07 October 2018